Itako

Virginia Aronson

Clare Songbirds Publishing House Poetry Series
ISBN 978-1-947653-91-7
Clare Songbirds Publishing House
Itako © 2020 Virginia Aronson

Cover image courtesy of Mel Goss © 2020

All Rights Reserved. Permission to reprint individual poems must be obtained from the author who owns the copyright.

Printed in the United States of America
FIRST EDITION

Clare Songbirds Publishing House was established to provide a print forum for the creation of limited edition, fine art from poets and writers, both established and emerging. We strive to reignite and continue a tradition of quality, accessible literary arts to the national and international community of writers, and readers. Chapbook manuscripts are carefully chosen for their ability to propel the expansion of art and ideas in literary form. We provide an accessible way to promote the art of words in order to resonate with, and impact, readers not yet familiar with the siren song of poets and writers. Clare Songbirds Publishing House espouses a singular cultural development where poetry creates community and becomes commonplace in public places.

140 Cottage Street
Auburn, New York 13021
www.claresongbirdspub.com

Contents

Itako Dying	6
The Trade	8
Itako Begins	10
Wedding Night	12
Itako Speaks	14
The Training	16
Unborn	18
Itako Ice Bucket Challenge	20
Two	22
Itako Dreams	24
Seer	26
You See Itako	28
Itako and You	30

The sun shone bright upon her when she spoke,
And yet her eyes received no ray of light.
—Charles Lamb

The only thing worse than being blind
is having sight but no vision.
—Helen Keller

Pleasure and pain are equal in a clear heart
no mountain hides the moon
—Ikkyu

Itako Dying

Ancient practices
wither and crumble
like everything green
and lush and alive
with desire.

Spirits live on
and the *itako*
who speak
to them, to you
are old, dead eyed
frail, still
blind.

You must visit them
a journey of trouble
to the northernmost place
on the main island
Mount Dread
volcanic
blackened
imposing itself
on you.

You will blush
shy from her
small hesitant steps
tiny whistling bird
in your uncalloused palm.

Do not look away
from her marbled eyes.
Step up and
speak!
She is here
to help you
find the love
she never had.

You must suffer
sight
not necessary
for seers.

Ancient Japanese believed blindness was a sign of spiritual powers. Itako *are blind women trained to communicate with the spirits of the dead.*

The Trade

The way breath
escapes lips
in a whoosh
a whistle
a laugh
a scream.

She knows what skin
feels like
remembers how green
the pines stood
stabbing the bleeding heart
of the lake blue sky
bright stars splashing down
around her upturned face.

She can no longer see
inside her mind
she sees everything.

Her parents mourn
what she has lost
they have lost
silently
the village whispers
barter hard
sell her
to the shamans
who train the blind.

She will leave home
with her buyers
ride a ribbed donkey
to the cold clear north
bend down
to the will
of her family
her people
her fate.

She's a child lost
a girl who kneels
a shadow in the crisp
sweet screaming air.

She will never see
she will see everything.

Itako *are dying off and the remaining practitioners number less than twenty, most old and frail. They live in Aomori, the northernmost prefecture on Japan's largest island, near Mount Osore, an idle volcano.*

Itako Begins

Three years—
a long time
without love.

      Three years
too long
to wear a ragged tunic
cower in fear
weep for rice.

      Three years
just long enough
to learn how to see
when your eyes are blind
your family far away
your young body
thin, blue and hollow
so full of longing.

      Three years
from eleven, twelve
to the ripe heart age
when the spirits come
and fill you with warm air.

      Three years
of ice water and bone freeze
hardened tears and empty fingers
bruises and pain and crackled skin
until you hear them speaking
and the rice cake bleeds

—and your life begins.

Itako *training is rigorous. It lasts three years and includes harsh living conditions, hunger, cold, and dousing with ice water many times a day.*

Wedding Night

Dress red as summer sunset
dress red as the morning
blood that will shed like tears
I cannot see
and I dream of red fish,
red rice
I can eat with my own hands
feel the grain grace my lips
the grit between my teeth

Tomorrow
I am marrying my *kami*
a spirit that loves me
despite my empty eyes
the dirt I cannot wash
the beauty I can only
feel with my fingers,
darting tongue, soft heart

open to my *kami*
I pray and dream and chant
all the bad years
until he comes to me
sad girl, bent over
shivering bones
the ice baths
bucket after bucket
on my shriveled
nakedness
until I drop ribs down
in the frozen mud

Tomorrow
I will marry my spirit
and the ceremony
food and feasting
the reward

clean red dress
the gift
my *kami*
takes me into arms
I cannot see
and holds me

in the prison of his love

After training is complete, a wedding ceremony is held in which the new itako *marries a* kami *(Shinto) spirit. This spirit will serve as her guide into the world of the dead.*

Itako Speaks

Blind from birth, sold
at thirteen and I can see
your dead baby
he is safe, he loves you
for letting him go to another
life. You can name him now
he has another name.

Blind from a fever
at ten I came here and
I can see your dead husband
he is happy, sends
love and the money hidden
under old paperwork
in his desk drawer.

Blind in one eye
the other veiled
in darkness and I can see
your dear mother
her crumpled bag face
alight with joy, knowing
you still mourn her.

Blind from birth
bad luck, poverty
girls sent away
to horror mountain
we live in the woods
come out once a year
like cherry blossoms, delicate
teens flowering
with sight.

Temple walls crumble
cracks widen
lava rocks underfoot
frail old women
now

we see ourselves
stagger slide
into the other world
with all your most prized
long lost
possessions.

In Japanese culture, volcanoes are where spirits of the dead wait for reincarnation. Once a year, itako *appear at the Obon festival near Mount Osore to provide spiritual guidance to those in need. Obon, held in July, is believed to be the time when the spirits of the dead return.*

The Training

Hold the baby like this
she moves my arms
I feel its warmth
soft and sweet
bread dough rising
in a fragile bowl.

Ready for the mothers
my *sensei* prods me
with roughhewn hands
here, there
just so
promises
to lead me
to spirit visions
to share with the grieving

Parents and grandparents
still weep for the lost
pray for the souls
kuchiyose
and I comfort them

Sing-chant, reach out
through the wispy mist
grasping for messages
from the unborn

here in the temple
of dread and doom
despair
all the blind girls
we hold our thin arms
just so

we will never see
our own babies there

For almost a thousand years, the Japanese have practiced kuchiyose, *ritual contact with the dead. At modern day Obon festivals, people wishing to contact deceased loved ones can pay around $30 for* itako *to communicate messages to and from their beloved dead.*

Unborn

The women gather round
some in designer finery, others
down at the heels hauteur
waiting for her to emerge
from the stone-age crumble
of the ancient temple.

Her cane crooked
as the thin bones
of her arching spine
she makes her way slowly
over rubble and lava rock
to her annual audience.

Despite her blindness
or because of it
her gaze could break glass
toothless mouth a dark chamber
of unspoken horrors
cool bald head
like an owl's egg.

Visitors flutter about
mouths moving
swollen eyes begging
for contact, information
some kind of impossible
love
an old blind woman
could never provide.

She will give them all
exactly
what they beg for
what they think
they desire.

They will return to their homes
their cars and computers
AC, heat and soft beds

itako to her darkness.

Visitors to itako *bring gifts of fruit and candy. They tell her the name of the deceased, the age, sex, and relationship.* Itako *calls on her* kami *by singing and chanting. She may call on* Jizo, *the protective spirit for the unborn.*

Itako Ice Bucket Challenge

Wooden pallets, wooden buckets, wooden faces
trainer shamans
and *itako*, girls
sad and sightless
and the sun beating down
pitiless as the older women
with rules and scorn, voices
like saws on crisp wood.

Endless winter
snow to wade through
sandaled feet, bare heads
hands like ice
buckets of ice
water
showering down
one after another
until the spirit leaves them

on the cold hard ground.

That's when *kami* comes
asks to live with you
for
ever
inside your fragile
bone chattering shell
your unseeing skull
and you say
yes.

You've been trained to say
yes.

Eyes and yes
are almost
the same word.

Itako *practice was established so that blind girls would have a purpose in life and be able to give back to their communities. In ancient times, a girl's village would pay for her training. After initiation, the new practitioner would be told she was no longer a burden to her people and would now be a contributing member of society.*

Two

She has two eyes
but cannot see them
each one a peeled grape
lizard egg
a soft baby bird
perched in her head
like a song of hope

And two ears
so she can hear
the *kami*, the spirits
voices from the borderlands
the unborn, the lost
wandering the countryside
invisible
like her
not seeing
like her
driven by love

Her two lips
pursed, soft
and her hot skin aches
for touch
the cool hands
of want

She has two hearts
beating in tandem
one inside the other
like a pebble in a fist

the tiny heart hidden
from her shaman
her *sensei*
the other *itako*

it flutters
bursts with longing

no one else
sees.

In 1875, when Japan was modernizing, itako *practice was outlawed. Practitioners were seen as con artists with the same social status as prostitutes.*

Itako Dreams

Alone
on the straw mat
on the cold slab
on the dirt floor
blank
eyes open
visions come
in warm colors.

The dream body
fits her
like a tailored suit
she wears out
like a woman
of the world
body free
to dance on smooth marble
lounge on velvet couches
love on thick fur rugs.

Awake
her brittle body
a test tube
a petri dish
an experiment in loss
at the mercy
of the spirits.

Asleep
the same body
a bright photograph
a shiny calendar
of better days
ahead.

The popularity of itako *increased after World War II when many Japanese wished to contact the war dead. Flocks of people still visit* itako. *Women often ask to communicate with infants lost through miscarriage, stillbirth, or from abortion.*

Seer

What name is on her lips
kami, Jizo, spirit
guide to the dark
unknown she waits before us
clawing animal bones, shells
while she leans in a cane tilt
toward the black crevices
in the moonish lava rock.

What images in her eyes
whited, sealed up
in bare rooms
down empty halls
blank walls of her own
mind the screen
without pink blossoms
deep blue ocean waves
plump fruit in pastel bowls
flush baby skin
the sparkle in dark eyes.

What voice in her ears
sounds tumbled like stones
scattered from the volcano
her own like an eagle
calling its mate
over long distances and
she speaks to those
we cannot hear
or see

but we want to
now
before we leave this world
for the one she slips in
and out of
like sandals
loose on small calloused feet

gnarled hands clutching bamboo
skulls and beads jangling
bone-white eyes wide,

seeing
what we cannot.

Itako *carry bamboo boxes filled with charms including animal skulls and teeth, jawbones from bear and fox, eagle claws, shells, and beaded necklaces.*

You See Itako

And her long distance eyes
cast you down the strange highway
to an unknown destination
you rush
to meet your beloved
in a borderland
a hidden world
not your own.

Her cloudy day eyes
settle like fog
on what you cannot see
shadows dancing
like car headlights
in misted woods
over rough trunks of trees
thick with survival
blinding white flashes
on blackest black.

Eyes distant running
a race in no place
as far as time travels
from a pocket watch
or the crash tide
from an angry sea,
your future
from your control
and
you

from the dead
who loved you

or not.

Itako *tradition is believed to have roots in the monk culture. Wives of traveling monks chanted and offered amulets for sale.*

Itako and You

Your body the saboteur
your mind the prison guard
and evictor as you wait
for *itako* magic, her
chanting, singing, begging
for your release

Through the transparent skin
of stretched thin time
past unseen barriers
her meatless shadow
dipping in and out of swatches
of a darkness that recedes
into itself and she
leaks and swirls, whipping

into you
like a steel pickaxe
blue toxic gas
a highwire cyclone
slapping and ripping away
that which binds us
to ourselves
and you struggle
to contain
your multitudes
but feel it all
give way

Until you flounder
in the density of otherness
lost in a green field
of empty rooms
running down endless halls
rockface, jagged and bleak
still locked inside
your crumbling fortress

Blind to your own
lack of sight.

Itako may soon disappear as young people no longer take on the tradition. In modern Japan, people who are vision impaired can be active members of society with education, families, and professional careers.

Virginia Aronson is the author of the chapbook *Tropical Diagnoses* (Finishing Line Press, 2011). She is the director of Food and Nutrition Resources Foundation, which published *Mottainai: A Journey in Search of the Zero Waste Life* (Dixi Books, UK, 2019). FNR supports individuals and organizations working to improve the broken food system, making healthy food available to all, enhancing food workers' rights, and teaching ways of feeding and eating that are good for people, animals, and the earth.

www.ingramcontent.com/pod-product-compliance
Lightning Source LLC
Chambersburg PA
CBHW062040120526
44592CB00035B/1816